Getting Y   H   Fi

G000152229

Your Ultimate Aim—A truly fit horse.

Flair IV, a brown, six year old mare by Right Flare, owned by Mr. L. Constance MRCVS is seen here returning from the Roads and Tracks, and Steeplechase Phases of the 1975 Wylye Horse Trials with an effortless, free stride, trotting on in perfect harmony with her rider, the Olympic Gold Medallist, Mrs. Bridget Parker, before going on to finish the best British entry in their Novice Section, having gone clear throughout.

Despite the pressures and stresses of a big competition, a horse should, as Flair IV did, remain calm and relaxed, while at the same time being capable of undertaking real work over a sustained period of time without undue fatigue or strain. This can only be achieved by slow, careful preparation in the early weeks, once truly fit they can be asked to work, but not before.

Getting your horse fit

DIANA R. TUKE

J. A. ALLEN & COMPANY LTD

1 Lower Grosvenor Place London SW1W 0EL

First published in 1977
by J. A. Allen & Co. Ltd.
1 Lower Grosvenor Place
London SW1W 0EL

Reprinted 1978
Reprinted 1981
Reprinted 1983

ISBN 0 85131 255 1

All the photographs
in this book were
taken by the author

British Library Cataloguing in Publication Data

Tuke, Diana
    Getting your horse fit.
    1. Horses — Handbooks, manuals, etc.
    1. Title
636.1'08'3   SF285.3

ISBN 0 85131 255 1

Printed in Great Britain by
Brown Knight & Truscott Ltd.

Contents

1. A good, sensible type of field shed—useful against flies in summer and bad weather in winter. Or, as in the photograph, for the dry storage of hay and straw.

CHAPTER 1

Care while resting

Every horse and pony requires a rest and holiday for part of the year. Some get it in the late autumn, others in the early summer. In the case of the former, if they have been stabled, rugged and possibly clipped, then they will require to sleep in by night—with a rug if necessary, and run out by day either without a rug, or if cold and wet, in a New Zealand rug. While those summering out, once the weather is settled and warm, can enjoy their freedom day and night till the flies get bad.

To feed a resting horse or pony depends on what keep—grass, you have available. Those resting in the winter will require hay—either fed in the field, or in the stable, and a feed of corn at least once a day to maintain condition and ward off the cold. Sometimes horses are turned out in winter to fend for themselves, this is cruel and foolish. Once flesh has been lost at this time of year it is hard to replace and damage to tissue and muscle formation is inevitable. Parasites like lice help to reduce the stamina of the unfortunate horse or pony.

Heat producing foods—oats, maize, cooked linseed or high protein nuts which will stoke up their internal heating system, thereby enabling them to keep warm, and to maintain condition, are needed. How much food depends on the weather and their size. A mild open winter will mean they can have a normal ration with *hay ad lib,* but hard weather will call for extra feeding, and in fact a large horse if forced to live out under such conditions, should receive more than if it were stabled and in work. Keeping a horse at grass in winter is certainly not a way to save expense, you may not have the straw, but you have far more expensive feed to buy.

It is far kinder and better for the horse (ponies if small and unclipped are different as they grow heavy coats) to let the horse sleep in with a good bed and run out by day either without a rug or with a New Zealand rug; in this way it can have a feed night and morning and a large hay net at night. Hay is saved this way as there is little or no wastage—out in the field waste is bound to occur to some extent.

If resting in Summer, the best time of the year, and normal for hunters, a horse in good condition requires no extra feeding if the grass is growing well. Very dry summers may mean feeding the horse once the initial flush of grass has gone from the field. Short grass is best and providing the field is kept clean—droppings should be picked up once or twice a day if possible (certainly in a small field) and the grass topped to remove the coarse grass that no horse or pony will eat, a fit, healthy horse or pony will do very well during May, June and July. After July the food value starts to drop in the grass and extra feeding is sometimes required either in the form of hay, or a small corn feed with salt and a supplement added to give it the required vitamins and minerals. By July too, the flies are getting bad and, unless the field has a good shed, the horse is better brought in during the heat of the day and given a feed if necessary or at least a small hay net. This has two advantages, one they are not stamping their feet and legs at the flies, thereby reducing the risk of laming themselves; secondly they are not blowing themselves out on grass that does not provide high food value.

Care & Management

Whether resting in winter or summer, water—clean, fresh and clear is their right and must be at hand all the time. Notice in very hot weather if the horses are bothering to come out and drink. Some horses hate the flies and would rather dry up than walk over to get a drink. In winter watch out for ice. In frosty weather ice on the water trough must be broken at least three times a day.

Feet are another area for concern with the resting horse or pony. More horses lame themselves at grass than is probably realized. Pick out feet every day and check for thrush (yes, it hits horses at grass as well as in the stable), chips to the wall and sandcracks can form. If shoes have been removed—it is best to remove them if possible for part of the time anyway as it allows the food to expand naturally, the feet must be rasped back to shape once every five weeks. Failure to do this is asking for trouble. A chip to the wall can be smoothed off by an experienced person with a rasp, this saves a broken foot. If the ground is hard, then front shoes may be required to protect the feet, and hind ones too, if the horse is out on its own. Horses out together should not have hind shoes on, a few are safe, but there is a serious risk of kicking. Un-shod feet can cut, but the damage is normally less.

Every day the horse or pony should be gone over very carefully for cuts, scratches, signs of lice or other mishap, like a lost shoe or raised clench. Any cut or scratch must be cleaned thoroughly and dressed—the cleaning and dressing being repeated every day till a full healing process has been achieved. To leave cuts and scratches only leads to unnecessary scars—scars that need never be. Also watch for signs of ill health—listlessness, coughing and other things that denote all is not well. If in doubt bring in and watch to see what develops. Send for professional help if the trouble does not clear in two to four days, or is known to be serious at the outset.

Before commencing a rest period, every horse or pony should be well wormed (or at least have an e.p.g. which is an egg count to determine if the horse or pony requires worming and if so how badly); have its teeth filed to remove any sharp edges; and receive any anti-tetanus injections if the horse or pony is not fully covered, also its flu. vac. boosters if due.

Providing reasonable care is taken and the horse or pony is not neglected it should settle down to a peaceful rest, coming up refreshed, ready to start getting fit again, once its holiday is over.

Remember though never to turn a horse or pony out in a field which has bad fencing—good, sound fencing is essential.

CHAPTER 2

Preparing to commence work

This booklet is principally concerned with getting horses fit, although ponies have to be got fit as well, and the principle is, on the whole, the same. The only difference is that a pony under 14 hands will get fit in a shorter time than a large hunter, providing it is not grossly fat when work commences. Its hard food intake too is less if being ridden by a child. Should the pony be required for hard work, like eventing, then it is wise to follow the routine set out for horses, and take the extra weeks to get the pony really hard and fit so that it can cope with the work involved.

Getting a horse fit takes a minimum of eight weeks, more if the horse is very large or over fat. In the case of over fat horses—those whose body outline is that of a square sided oblong, the first two weeks of the getting fit process will have to be extended to four or five weeks in bad cases, and the next two weeks also doubled before faster work is permitted.

When to get a horse up to start its preparation depends largely on what you require the horse for. Those doing only light hacking will not require the same high protein diet as those being prepared for hunting, eventing, show jumping, long distance riding, polo, racing, or any other competitive sport requiring a really fit horse. Pony trekking and sponsored rides also require a fit horse, but they must remain quiet and suitable for their riders. Light hacking requires the first five weeks of the programme, after which it can level out. For the rest the getting fit process will take a minimum of eight weeks, and for some ten-twelve weeks, after which they should be fit and hard enough to undertake real work that calls on them to use themselves to the full over a sustained period of time.

With an experienced horse whose training has been completed, this time should be enough before a competition, but with a young horse who must undergo a period of training to bring it up to competition standard, then whatever extra time you feel necessary to achieve this must be added to the eight weeks.

Preliminary Considerations
There are two schools of thought as to whether a horse should be

brought into the stable and never let out again, or whether it is kinder and just as good to stable it part of the time, while still letting it have a certain amount of time at grass, decreasing the time at grass as the exercise and getting fit process progresses.

The first case is sometimes necessary if getting fit is started after Christmas, as in the case of eventers being brought up for the spring events; or long distance competitors who are aiming at the spring rides. The second though is useful for those brought up in the summer or autumn, and has the advantage that during the first four weeks the horse can work off its freshness by a canter or buck, without risking a rebuke from its rider!

If I am bringing a horse up in mid-June then I like to stable it by day and turn it out by night if the weather is suitable. It is cooler then and they are away from the flies by day. I bring them in at 5 am and ride from 6 am to 7 am or 7.30 am, according to how long I am giving them. It is the only time they will walk quietly in the summer, and they can then receive their feeds in the stable during the day.

Diet
Before commencing work certain preparations are necessary. I like to start feeding my horses before bringing them into work if I have to get them up to competition fitness in eight weeks. At least, if they start at about five pounds of corn, I like to work up to this amount slowly over the preceding seven to ten days as it is very bad to just offer any horse a full ration at once. Horses that have been fed while at rest do not require this pre-feeding as they are receiving it already.

Care & Management
During this pre work week the horse must be shod. Telephone or write a card to your blacksmith at least two to three weeks before you wish the first set of shoes put on—old shoes may go back in many cases if enough wear is left for a month's slow work, and give him the date you wish to have the horse shod. With luck you will get it done on time.

Watch your horse being shod if possible, and note the condition of its feet once pared back into shape. Look out for any tell tale red patches near the heels, this could mean old trouble, or trouble brewing. Corns and bruises cause a lot of lameness and a horse can bruise a foot at grass as easily on a stone as when stabled.

If old shoes have been put back, then take the horse out for a short walk in hand or under saddle to round off the heads of the nails before leaving it loose in the field. Sharp edges can cut, and no one wants cuts at this stage.

The horse will also have to be wormed if the worming routine of your stable dictates this. Much better to do it before the horse starts work than when it is working. No horse with a worm burden can be got truly fit, so it behoves the owner to see that the horse is clear.

Teeth are another point—some horses whose teeth were bad before being turned out may require checking again, and if necessary filing. Sharp teeth only lead to bad digestion of food and fussing over the bit. Poor condition is often caused by teeth and not worms or lice, though these of course are factors too, and cause lack of condition.

A bad infestation of lice can take a pint of blood a day off their hosts!

Worms are often deceptive in as much as they have a habit of not always reducing the host to skin and bone until they are well established. Some horses I have known have been over fat in their stomachs and found to carry burdens of 4,000 or more, which is very heavy. So however well the horse looks, have an e.p.g. done at regular intervals.

We now come to the question of wearing a roller in the stable, the object of which is to harden the skin where the girth goes. I personally have never done this, nor found it necessary. Far better groom your horse and get it clean—dirt rubs and causes girth galls. Hard tack too, is another prime cause. All tack must be scrupulously clean and as soft as possible—supple tack does not rub or cause friction like hard stuff. Remember to tighten one's girth carefully and pull the forelegs gently forward by placing a hand behind the knee, before leaving the stable, to remove all the wrinkles of skin and lay the hair of the coat flat. A loose girth only rubs.

If the summer weather is really warm, then a bath carefully carried out, using warm water and a good Animal Shampoo, is a help to clean the skin, and remove the grit and dirt which always collects in the coat when they are running out. Before washing the horse should be brushed for a few days to remove any loose coat.

Horses brought back into work in the winter are treated differently. Once they have started work they must be clipped and given a full compliment of rugs. Chaser clip—head, neck (lower half) and tummy being clipped, while the top of the back is left on—is a useful clip to start with for well bred horses as they are less inclined to chills during the slow work period. They can be fully clipped later on before competing if required. Once clipped they will all require a rug under their saddles for exercise. They must be kept warm.

Rugging in summer is not necessary until the horse is doing fast work and made to sweat, then they should have a light one at

2. Galavant—February 1975, in fit, hard condition. This photograph shows how a Chaser clip should be done—a useful clip on a well-bred horse to prevent chilling.

night. On hot nights in summer it can be put on last thing at dusk and removed at early morning stables for the day. In cooler weather they can wear one all the time if necessary. Too hot is as bad as too cold.

The long process of getting fit is necessary to convert flab into muscle and enable the horse to perform without harm to limbs, wind or heart, and give of its best when the big question is asked.

CHAPTER 3

First week

Some people now reckon to ride without shoes to start with around the fields. This is not very wise, for one thing no horse will walk quietly on grass; and for another it does not harden their legs; and to let them trot and canter as some advocate is all wrong, they must walk for at least two weeks before doing anything else.

Exercise
How far to go? This is a good question. A horse straight off grass and from a long rest—therefore absolutely soft, will only require about twenty minutes the first day. Half-an-hour at the most. They may appear gay and keen to go on, but they must be restrained and made to walk. They will settle in a day or two! The reason for this necessity to walk is that the horse's muscles must adjust themselves to the weight of the rider and a saddle clamped on their back. Their centre of balance is altered and if allowed to go at fast paces the tendons and ligaments may over stretch and not return to normal—result, a strained tendon, and or, ligament, trouble only too well known, alas.

If the horse has been fed before coming up, then the very short ride of fifteen to twenty minutes can be increased fairly quickly, and in most cases be started at the half-hour with safety. By the end of the first week the horse should be capable of walking steadily for an hour; and at the end of the ride be willing still to walk out well and not be drooping along with its head on the ground or beating it up and down. Never over do the horse at this stage, this is when the trouble starts—stumbles that lead to falls, and strained tendons and ligaments from sudden jarring as a toe is caught in the ground. Do not slop along, but make the horse carry itself, and keep alert yourself to hold it together if a joint should 'buckle', that is, give slightly, which can happen with an unfit horse. Dragging feet are no good to either the horse or its feet— they must be made to pick them up and put them down firmly.

Diet
With work comes food—the two go hand-in-hand. Throughout the next eight weeks and beyond, food must match work. More

15

work, more food, and once work moves into the medium or heavy category, the food must be of the high protein type. A low protein diet is only suitable for light work such as hacking, when the horse is required to be sober. It can be used, if necessary, during the first four weeks, but certainly not afterwards if the horse is going to be called on to really work.

Light work is one hour per day; *medium* is about one-and-a-half to two hours of not too hard work; and *heavy* is anything over this, or those who pack into a one-and-a-half to two hour stint a great deal of hard work. Thirty—forty minutes of hard schooling is worth two hours of hacking, or thereabouts. So it is the type of work that counts as well as the time taken.

A small horse of 15 hands will require overall less food for the same work, than a large one of 16 hands plus. And the very big fellows, who range from 17 hands to even over 18 hands in a few cases, will consume even more. A big framed horse on short legs will require more than a small horse of the same height. Therefore a large bodied 15 hands one will eat as much as a light-framed 15.3 hands or 16 hands horse.

When feeding remember a horse's stomach for its size is small, and lies next to its diaphragm—too much bulk and the pressure on the diaphragm is increased cutting down the room for lung expansion and this in turn leads to bad breathing and damaged lungs. Cut down the power of breathing freely and a strain is then imposed on the heart that lies to the left hand side of the chest, just in front of where the girth goes. Heart strength lies in the muscle power of the horse—the heart being after all a lump of muscle that acts as a pump for circulating the blood round the body. Poor muscle, poor heart function; this in turn leads to a strain on the heart and trouble. To build up muscle, protein is required, plus the necessary vitamins and minerals to ensure health. These alone though will not produce hard, strong muscles that ripple when a horse moves, beneath a soft, silky skin and shining coat, unless the horse has the correct amount of sound, sensible exercise and thorough grooming. The three go together.

The fitter the horse the less bulk food it requires and more 'short' feed, that is feed that is packed with energy producing nourishment. Oats, high protein nuts, high protein milk pellets, maize, linseed—these are all energy producing foods; whereas spring grass and hay, though rich in protein, are bulk foods and therefore not sufficient to get a horse fit on. Grass in winter has no real food value and poor hay has none either. When getting a horse fit always feed only the best, and feed little and often rather than one large feed.

The following chart gives the approximate average weight of a horse or pony, and its daily required total intake of food. Remember, though, size versus weight is not always accurate—a 14 hand show pony will weigh considerably less than a 14 hand Welsh Cob, so it is the size of the body not the length of the legs that support it that really counts. If in any doubt try and get your horse or pony put over a weighbridge, or ask your veterinary surgeon to give his estimate as to approximate weight—it is after all required for worming as well as feeding.

Bodyweight versus daily food requirements

Size (Hands)	Average approximate Bodyweight	Daily Food Intake
13 hh	500 lbs	12½ lbs
13.2 hh	600 lbs	15 lbs
14 hh	700 lbs	17½ lbs
14.2 hh	800 lbs	20 lbs
15 hh	950 lbs (T.B.)	23¾ lbs
15 hh	1,100 lbs (Hunter)	27½ lbs
15.2 hh	1,000 lbs (T.B.)	25 lbs
15.2 hh	1,250 lbs (Hunter)	31¼ lbs
16 hh	1,100 lbs (T.B.)	27½ lbs
16 hh and over	1,400 lbs (Hunter)	35 lbs

All in all, diet plays a large part in getting any horse fit. To live at all they require a certain amount, but to work they must receive basically 2½% of their bodyweight in food—that is 25 lbs of food for every 1,000 lbs of bodyweight; hard work or breeding stock will burn up more food, so rations in these cases may be higher, but remember, horses and ponies are highly individual and each must be fed as such.

Most rations relate to dry matter—hay (when hay alone is being fed the moisture content must be taken into consideration, 19½ lbs of hay giving 17 lbs dry matter); oats; barley; flaked maize; nuts (here the protein content varies and the higher the fibre content, the lower the protein content in most cases); bran; high protein milk pellets (a useful means of increasing the protein content of the feed without undue extra bulk); sugar beet pulp or nuts (before being soaked—both MUST be soaked for 24 hours before being fed); these are all dry matter.

Grass has a high moisture content and therefore a horse or pony will require far more to obtain the necessary dry matter for its needs. Grass is only used as a maintenance ration and is no good to get a horse or pony fit on.

Concentrates (corn and high protein foods) are essential for any horse or pony in serious work, but a certain amount of roughage is also essential for digestion. So, though the rule is to decrease the bulk (roughage) foods as the concentrates are increased with increased work, the roughage must never be reduced beyond roughly the 40 (roughage)—60 (concentrates) ratio. Part of the roughage can be fed as 'choppy' (chaff or chopped hay) and mixed in the feeds, and sugar beet once soaked also produces roughage, so its feeding value comes into both groups, though never over feed it and only as a very small part of any diet.

Water is another essential. Clean, fresh water must be available at all times in the field and the stable—buckets being changed up to five or six times a day. No horse likes stale water; without water no horse can do well and be a credit to its owner.

From the time the horse comes in it must be thoroughly strapped every day. This helps to build up the muscles which, to start with, will be soft and podgy in the region of the shoulder and hindquarters, and along the crest of the neck. Once fit the horse should be hard. Its shoulder muscles are very important as the horse has no collar bone, and relies on its muscles to hold its forelegs onto its body! Quite a thought. A horse in poor condition will have no flesh to convert into muscle. This has to be built up at the same time, the diet being adjusted accordingly and the extra flesh producing foods added.

CHAPTER 4

Second week

At the end of every working week the horse will require one day's rest to relax. During the early weeks this can be just a day in the field if stabled at night; if it is very hot the horse should be let out when it is cooler. A day off with a walk in hand, grazing, is best for those stabled all the time. This in-hand grazing walk should last a minimum of twenty minutes and not more than forty. At least one rug is required on a clipped horse, or more if the weather is cold. Which day of the week this rest comes on depends on the owner's other commitments. For some Sunday is the only day they can really ride their horse, if so, then rest the horse on Monday, and work the weekly programme accordingly.

Exercise
Having completed the first week's walking, the horse should now be ready to start the second. Fresh from a day off, it should set off feeling bright and eager. All the same it should have now settled to its routine and be willing to walk properly. This is the frame of mind we must get the horse into—fooling about does it no good and is unacceptable. Longer rides can now start and a full six to eight mile circuit lasting an hour-and-a-quarter to an hour-and-a-half can be tried. Do not aim at the full distance the first day, but by the middle of the week the horse should be returning to the stable as fresh as it left it and by the end of the second week have ceased to puff at the walk, and be capable of walking out for the whole ride.

Roads with good surfaces are best for walking exercise and quiet lanes that have sound going. Slithering along from rut to rut is not good and should be avoided in the early weeks. If the horse is calm and willing to walk, and a freshly combined field is available, the horse might be allowed to walk across it to give change of scene, this often links up another new ride. But on no account let the horse trot or canter yet.

Care & Management
Back in the stable each day look carefully for signs of rubbing from tack, and check the legs for any signs of heat or swelling. The

shoes should also be checked for risen clenches—and the feet for bruising or splitting. Care should be exercised to pick out the feet thoroughly. This checking is essential if trouble is to be spotted in its early stages. With luck, at this stage all should be well.

The corners of the mouth and bars must be watched—these can rub or crack if care is not exercised to sponge out the corners to remove slobber. Sore mouths once established are hard to heal unless the bit is removed.

If the mouth is getting sore, rub a light coating of vaseline in the corners to prevent cracking and in bad cases ride without a bit. Now this is not easy. A hackamore is one answer, also a bitless bridle can be made up. A lungeing cavesson with the reins attached to the side rings and passing back through a fairly short running martingale has answered, even on a fit horse. But care must be taken to ensure you are under control if you are riding in traffic. I have, in fact, gone for a cross-country ride jumping tacked up like this on a fit Thoroughbred, so it does work.

Grooming now should be showing results and the horse's coat getting a true shine on it, and all the old dead coat giving way to new underneath. Manes, tails and heels should have been trimmed to remove excess hair. Tails will take at least a fortnight to re-gain a good shape as one cannot pull them too hard all at once, and the new short hair must come through before all the over-long hair is removed. Nevertheless, a tidy effect should have resulted by the end of the second week.

Diet

Corn will have been increased during the first part of the week, by approximately 1 lb—½ lb the first day and the rest the next. A 15 hand horse can now have 3 lbs a day, assuming it started at 2 lbs. If it started at 3 lbs, then it will now be receiving 4 lbs a day. A sixteen hand horse will have started at 5 lbs a day, and now be receiving 6 lbs, divided into three feeds. The smaller horse might have managed on two feeds a day, but now requires three. Bran in each case will be in the region of ½ lb per feed. Choppy (chaff or chopped hay, they are all the same and not to be mistaken for 'chaff' the cavings from thrashed corn, which is not suitable), is also added to each feed at the rate of two to four handfuls to give body to the feed and stop the bolting of corn.

Corn, strictly speaking, refers to Maize (Indian Corn), but in the context used here it refers to all grain fed to the horse—oats, barley, flaked maize, and horse nuts of different grades. So if a horse is receiving both oats and nuts, then the corn ration of 6 lbs could be 4 lbs oats and 2 lbs nuts; or, 6 lbs nuts and no oats. If low protein nuts are being fed and not high protein ones, then the 6 lbs rations must be increased to 9 lbs to give the same food value. I prefer a mixed diet and always feed oats, with high protein nuts added to boost up the value of the ration after the horse has been back in work about three to four weeks.

The vitamin and mineral supplement, which has been started gradually, must now be increased to the full recommended amount.

Before moving on to the next stage a look at the rough food guide might be in order to let us plan the weeks leading up to true fitness. The chart is for a sixteen hand horse of Thoroughbred type. A horse of fifteen hands will require less hay and the concentrate ration can stop increasing at the 7 lbs-10 lbs stage for the remaining weeks, unless the horse can take more. The smaller horse will start at 2 lbs-3 lbs per day, against the 5 lbs per day for the sixteen hand one. Big horses over sixteen hands will require overall more food per day and be increased at about 1 lb a week extra.

Progressive feeding chart

Week	1	2	3	4	5	6	7	8	9	10	11	12
Hay (including Choppy)	22½	21½	20½	19½	17	16	15	14	13	12	11	10
Concentrate Ration	5	6	7	8	9	10	11	12	13	14	15	16
Bran	1½	1½	1½	1½	2	2	2	2	2	2	2	2
Total	28	28	28	28	28	28	28	28	28	28	28	28
No. Feeds per day	3	3	3	3	4	4	4	4	4	4	4	4

Let them eat as much hay as they wish providing they are clearing their concentrate ration. If they are not, then cut back the hay till they are clearing everything. Horses are highly individual and no two rations will be quite the same. One horse can take 16 lbs of corn, whereas another can go silly on only 8 lbs-10 lbs. So use your judgement and stop increasing the hard food when the horse starts to act the fool. 12 lbs-14 lbs is the normal amount for the average horse, larger amounts are only for racehorses and three-day eventers with good, experienced riders on their backs. Long distance riders should only feed this rate if they are capable of coping with a fresh horse, and are really good riders.

After the fourth week only feed nuts of the 14%-16% protein group; ordinary horse and pony nuts only contain 10% protein, and high fibre content, which is no good for getting a horse truly fit. A protein supplement can be added, like milk pellets which will carry protein of up to 23% or thereabouts and also has a high oil content.

Other principal feeding stuffs are:

Oats—use only the best. These are fed either whole, bruised (cracked), or if the horse prefers, crushed, but this form is bulkier. Boiled (whole or bruised, soaked overnight and cooked next day) help to put on flesh.

Barley—boiled it is a good flesh producer, but I do not favour its use as part of the diet normally. It can be used crushed, but its principle use is to produce butcher ready cattle and pigs, and our horses are required to gallop and jump over an extended length of time—overladen inside with fat, they will blow up. Nuts carry a certain amount of barley so the horse receives all it requires from its nuts.

Flaked Maize—excellent in winter or when in hard work. Feed at about ½ lb per day for a small horse. Introduce about the 4th week.

Linseed—excellent for those in hard work or in winter. Feed as a Linseed mash once a week; or in the evening feed about twice a week. Soak overnight and then bring to the boil before simmering all day.

Black Treacle—used in each feed at the rate of one teaspoonful mixed in warm water to damp the feed.

Sugar Beet pulp and nuts—widely used, giving a source of sugar and fibre. Can replace choppy to a large extent, but the two can be fed together if required. Useful for big bodied, hungry horses; or fussy feeders. Soak overnight and use next day. Soak only enough for one day's use. Wash all buckets used for soaking each day and never have sour sugar beet hanging around. The pulp or nuts will at least treble itself during soaking, so ensure it soaks up all the water it can take before being fed, NEVER feed dry, if it expands inside the horse the horse could die!

Carrots—excellent as an extra. Feed about 1 lb per day—sliced lengthwise.

Salt—essential to every horse. Feed 1 oz per day.

3. Sensible, sound feeding is essential for getting a horse fit and maintaining it so. This photograph shows the principal feeding stuffs, together with equipment necessary for feeding.

Left to right: Net containing good quality seed hay; High Protein/Vitamin/Mineral Milk Pellet supplement; a comprehensive Vitamin/Mineral supplement; Black Treacle, together with a measuring jug to mix it in; a plastic bucket of the type suitable for mixing feeds and making mashes in; unsoaked Linseed in a 4 oz cream carton that makes a handy measure; heavy duty scales for weighing all feeds; a scoop (measure or dipper) for picking up feeding stuffs; in which are some Carrots, sliced lengthwise to prevent choking.

Front row: Bran; Flaked Maize; Oats; Nuts; behind: Choppy (Chaffed hay) also Mollassine Meal; and lastly unsoaked Sugar Beet Pulp.

4. Sugar Beet Pulp (or Nuts) MUST always be soaked for 24 hours before being fed. This photograph shows the dry Sugar Beet Pulp in a plastic bag before water is added.

5. At least twice the quantity of water is then added. A plastic bag was used so that I could photograph the expansion of the pulp, normally it is soaked in a bucket; in this case the beet can be seen floating in the water which has creased the bottom of the bag.

6. 24 hours later—The sides of the bag are now stretched straight by the expanded beet pulp. Fully soaked, it has taken up nearly all the water and risen slightly above the water line. NEVER FEED UNSOAKED SUGAR BEET PULP OR NUTS—IT CAN AND WILL KILL.

Remember the rules of feeding. Always water before feeding. Feed little and often. Weigh all food to ensure the horse is receiving the correct amount. This is essential as too little is as bad as too much, and in these days of high costs it is foolish to waste good food. Never work a horse on a full stomach, small feeds require an hour to digest, large ones two hours.

All mangers should be cleaned out thoroughly once a day, and buckets, etc., used for feeding rinsed after every feed. Sour food leads to bad doers. Feeding is an art, an art that can be acquired if one bothers. One person can give a feed and the horse eat up and do well, another can feed the same food with adverse effects. If you want a fit horse, then you must learn to become a first class feeder, if you are not one already.

CHAPTER 5

Third week

Well, those two vital first weeks of walking are at last behind us. But do not get excited. Although trotting can now be introduced into the programme, we must start carefully. Trotting jars the horse's legs and whole frame if indulged in to excess before the hardening process has been completed. Not that this means one can 'bash on' along the road or on hard going, even when the horse is fit. Trotting should always be done at an even pace which is less jarring, and a long stride is better for their legs than a short stabbing one that strikes into the ground.

Exercise
When the horse has had a day off, the first day's trotting must be confined to very short spells. One telegraph pole to the next and then walk again. At first you will find the horse only too willing to lapse back into a walk. Only start trotting after having walked the first half mile—a rule to be followed always. Never rush out and start trotting immediately as the horse must warm its muscles up first. Fail to do this and trouble will eventually follow sooner or later—sooner in most cases!

By the end of this first day's exercise which includes trotting the horse can have done about three to four short trots—and I mean short.

Day two will see the horse able to trot for slightly longer spells—four spells of one to two telegraph poles is enough. By the end of the week the horse should not be feeling tired at the end of its ride. If the roads on which you exercise have sound verges, then it is a good thing to trot on these at least part of the time, or along the side of a hedge if the field has good going. But watch it in the fields as this is an invitation to break into a canter, and no cantering can be allowed for another week yet.

Lungeing
You may have noticed no mention of lungeing has taken place so far, this is intentional. Lungeing normally means trotting, and until the horse is ready to trot, I do not like to lunge, hence the

reason it has not been included until the third week. Lungeing puts a certain strain on the horse until the muscles have stretched themselves in the required ark necessary to circle. Walking on the lunge the first day is best, if the horse will do so, otherwise confine the lungeing to five minutes each way. As the days progress, so too can the time spent lungeing. Never exceed fifteen minutes during the first week and split this into three spells of two-and-a-half minutes each way. One must stretch the muscles of the back evenly.

Lungeing is excellent as it not only supples the horse but also settles it. NEVER lunge off the bit—many do and this is how good mouths soon become bad mouths. Buy a proper lungeing cavesson and lunge off the centre nose ring which is on a swivel. One has far more control and can lead the horse round into a true circle more easily. Do not use side reins in the early stages as this puts too much strain on the neck and back muscles. With a newly broken horse, naturally it will have been lunged before starting ridden work, but we are talking of the broken horse coming back into work.

When to lunge is the next point. Most people believe in carrying out their lungeing before ridden work. I personally do not favour this, to lunge and then ride puts too much strain on an unfit horse. I like to exercise first and school in the morning, and then lunge after lunch. This splits up the exercise and does not tire the horse. Its muscles have been limbered up in the morning, rested, then worked in gently again. In this way the horse can have one-and-a-half hours in the morning, and another half-hour in the afternoon—two hours in all.

Schooling
Schooling too, can start now and a little slow trotting on large circles—no sitting trot work until the horse is much harder, this is how backs are strained. Just slow rhythmic trotting to the right and left. This type of schooling can be carried out during the morning exercise if a suitable place could be found that is quiet and has good sound going.

Care & Management
Up till now if the getting fit process has been in the middle of summer, the horse can have been sleeping out. Now it is necessary to bring it in each night. Give it a good deep bed of clean straw—

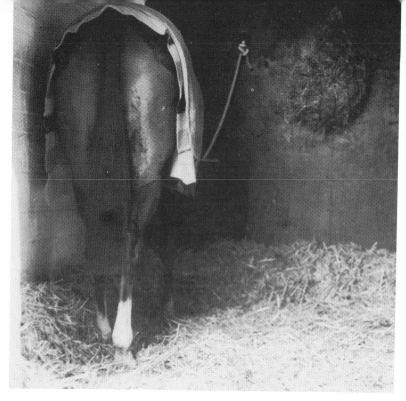

7. A good bed is essential—clean, ample wheat straw, banked well up against the walls to protect the horse's legs, and prevent the risk of chills from draughts or the horse getting cast; and at the same time level in the centre. Good, warm, clean rugs and blankets are also essential in winter on a clipped or part clipped horse—both are seen here. Note too, the correctly tied haynet and boxed in manger for safety.

wheat, or if the horse eats its bedding, peat or sawdust should be used. A good bed is essential as the horse must rest well at night and a shortage of bedding only leads to slipping in the box and the risk of injury. Bedding also creates warmth and warmth is necessary for muscle tone.

Routine is the next item to be worked out once the horse is sleeping in. In high summer it pays to ride before breakfast, not after, as it is much cooler and the morning sees the countryside at its best. Even towns are nicer early before the traffic rush is on. There is something special about the countryside at 5.30 am or 6 am. The wildlife should be about, and the dewy cobwebs give a fairy world feeling. If one has to do the slow work, then one might as well get the most enjoyment out of it.

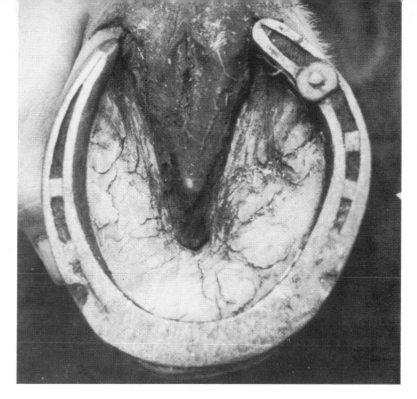

8. Watch out for the fullering wearing out—this shoe on the off-hind had been on four weeks and was about to be renewed. Note how the foot has grown leaving the shoe short at the heel, and how the thin shoe at the toe has removed protection from the sole. The road stud in this photograph had done four lots of shoeing—four months and about 1,000 miles! This is a healthy foot with a good frog.

Feed the horse on its return, then let it run out for two hours until the flies get bad. Bring it back into the stables, groom, and then give mid-day feed before leaving to rest and digest it.

About 3 pm, if one is free then, later otherwise, tack up and lunge for twenty minutes. Feed again about 7 pm after the horse has had another two hours in the paddock from 5 pm to 7 pm. This gives it only four hours out compared with at least twelve during the last two weeks. By cutting the grass intake—which incidently has up till now formed part of the dry matter intake— we will reduce the tendency to blow out and therefore enable the body to tighten up and start to tune up.

Watch for the shoes wearing out, once the fullering has gone. Telephone the blacksmith or drop him a card and get booked in

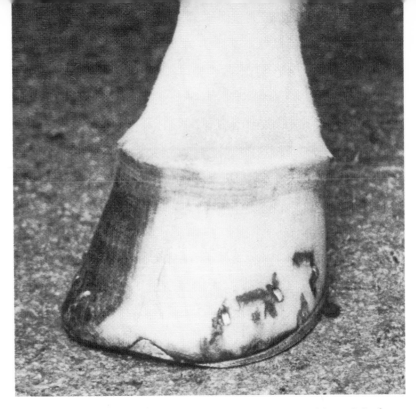

9. The off-fore waiting to be re-shod—the toe has worn thin and the foot started to over-grow the shoe. The two cracks in the inside of the foot were caused when the coronet was knocked in an accident 10 months before; note how the ends have been sealed with a hot iron to prevent further cracking of the horn.

so that he will be prepared to renew the shoes at the end of four weeks, or beginning of five. To let the feet overgrow is dangerous, it puts an unnecessary strain on the tendons and ligaments, also over-long feet lead to stumbling.

Pay attention to small details and the others will take care of themselves to a large extent.

CHAPTER 6

Fourth week

On the day following the rest day at the end of the third week, the concentrate ration can be increased—give half the extra amount in the evening feed and the rest the next morning. Never increase a food ration in one fell swoop. On the rest day the concentrate ration must now be reduced slightly following a bran mash the previous evening. When not working the concentrate ration must be reduced to avoid over heating the horse's system. Work and hard food must always go hand in hand.

Exercise

From the work point of view the horse should be having a minimum of an hour-and-a-half, and two hours for preference. This two hours can either be split into schooling, lungeing and road work, or be entirely road work.

Road work must be steady and progressive. The trots are now more frequent and for longer spells. Hills too, come into the programme now. Start to look for rides that have ever increasing slopes. Gentle ones to start with, getting steeper as the days go by. Walk up them briskly first, then start trotting up them carefully. At first the horse will probably start blowing half way up and try to walk—let it. It is fatal to push a horse at this stage; they know when they have had enough. By the end of the fourth week a horse who has had a progressive getting fit routine should be able to trot up a reasonable slope if not too long or steep. This trotting and walking up hills is the best thing in the world for building up the muscles of the hindquarters and back. Without these muscles being strong and well developed no horse can work really well. Strong hindquarters are essential for speed and jumping, as well as for accurate dressage. This hill work also builds up their lung power and gives them stamina.

Coming down hills try and avoid letting the horse slip, an all too easy occurrence on bad road surfaces; if the surface is good, then the horse should walk out down hill as well and freely as it does going up.

Care & Management

Stable routine by now will have settled down. Depending on the time of year, the morning stables can now be done before going out if it is too dark to exercise before breakfast; otherwise do the horse over and then exercise, feeding on return. This exercise must be early though, breakfast must not be delayed too long, otherwise the other feeds will not fit in easily. Up to the first of September it is possible to go out before breakfast, after that it is getting too dark to be back by 8 am, the latest one should feed. Once the change comes, feed at 6.15 am to 6.30 am and go out about 8 am till around 10 am. This then gives time for two hours in the paddock before their mid-day feed.

I do not intend going into full stable routine here, as I have already done it in depth in *Horse by Horse,* which is a guide to equine care in every aspect of the job. This booklet is intended as an enlargement on an important subject, for which space was necessarily restricted in the book itself. Attention must also be paid to bits and saddles so that one can get the best out of one's horse for the work required of it. Badly fitting, or incorrect saddles and bridles only hamper one's efforts to produce the finished article to the highest standard. *Bit by Bit* a guide to equine bits, and *Stitch by Stitch,* a guide to equine saddles, covers both these subjects with the same depth as the other book. As all three are fully illustrated, it is possible to learn what is required and thereby save hours of wasted time besides, I hope, many disappointments.

By the completion of the fourth week the horse should be beginning to harden up and the muscles on its shoulders and quarters be developing. The crest of the neck will be losing that feeling of a limp cod and be instead gaining a feel of solidity into which one's fingers cannot be pressed.

Even though the horse may now feel fit and be all eager to go on, one must not give in to either its wish or one's own, and start working properly. One has only reached the halfway stage and things can, if rushed at this stage, go wrong very easily. This is when wind and heart can be strained if the horse is allowed to over exert itself.

Only the foolish will take an unfit horse to competitions, or go cubbing. Many do, and it is very wrong. Even cubbing calls for more energy than many realize. Not only is the horse left standing at the covertside for long spells in the early morning—super on a nice morning, though not so good for the horse in wind, rain and early morning frost as so often occurs. Also there are those sharp gallops from one end of a covert to the other when one is asked to go to a special place. These gallops can do untold harm and may even cost one the season's hunting if one has only one horse! No, wait for even a short morning's cubbing (or showing) till the horse has done about six weeks' work. Even then one should only take the type of horse that can be made three-quarters fit in the time.

Those who have a horse shod one day and go out cubbing the next need their heads seeing to—cubbing is not the way to get your horse fit or to stay sound for the whole season. If hounds do come round your way leave your horse at home and go out on foot, this will get you fit and give your horse a chance to get fit in its own time.

Fitness of Rider
A word here about getting oneself fit may not be out of place. It is no good having your horse brought back into condition and made fit if you yourself are not fit enough to ride it correctly. If possible the rider who is going to hunt, show or event the horse should be the one to get it fit (unless they are riding every day on some other horse). This will ensure that by the time the horse is fit so too will they be. A rider flopping about in an unfit condition in the saddle for long periods only goes to making the horse's back sore, and if the horse should stumble then they are probably too unfit to be able to keep it on its feet.

If one has ridden the horse through its first four weeks, then even if one was unfit before one should be as fit as the horse now, and ready for the next stage.

CHAPTER 7

Fifth week

Exercise

Well, the halfway mark has now been reached, and providing the horse has come through this without sign of strain to its legs and is breathing freely and well at the trot, then it can be allowed to have a short, very slow canter during the commencement of its fifth week. Choose a field that has really good going—with a fair covering of grass, or else a stubble field free from holes and stones that has plenty of give in it without being slippery. Walk the first half mile or so; trot for a reasonable spell; walk again for an equal spell and then start trotting again in the given field; once settled, squeeze gently with your legs and push the horse into a balanced, slow canter. Avoid any fuss and make sure it does not rush off madly. Canter only for a short spell and ease gently back into a trot and then walk. Make all transitions smoothly, so avoiding the risk of strain caused by sudden change of pace.

No doubt you and the horse enjoyed that first canter a lot, and may be the horse showed its pleasure by giving a buck. If it did do not be too hard on it—not at this stage anyway. Sit tight and check it gently. Bucking is caused in an unfit horse by two things: one, they feel good and wish to say so; the other is that they feel some pain from their back muscles and are merely trying to stretch them. By the end of the week, unless prone to bucking, they should have settled down except for the odd buck.

How much to let a horse buck is a good question. Never, if you can help it let it give more than one (two at the most), for it can quickly become a habit if encouraged. Encouraging is quite another thing to being harsh with a horse for merely trying to relieve the pain in its muscles. As soon as the first buck has come out, get its head up without being rough and push it on with your legs, this will tend to raise the forehand and make it far harder for the horse to get its head down to buck. Never in the early canters let the horse canter on a loose rein, this merely asks for trouble and the rider deserves all he gets. Most horses when checked, if one says *no* firmly, will stop and drop back to the proper pace. A smack on the shoulder with a 'fish' tail ended stick will also let the horse know that bucking is not included in its programme.

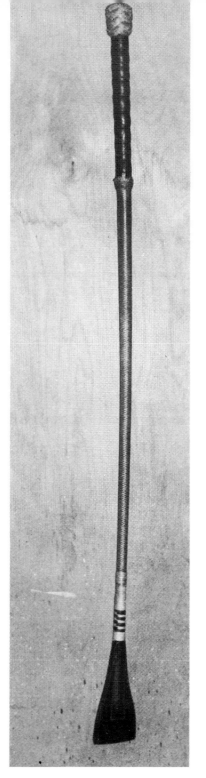

10. A "Fish Tail" ended whip or stick—a humane stick for correcting a horse when it misbehaves or for guiding it.

11. New shoes—Near-fore re-shod so that the shoe fits the foot. Note the careful bevelling of the hoof where it meets the shoe to prevent cracking of the horn; also the well turned clenches, centre toe clip and careful rasping of the wall, which has been kept low down and to the minimum. This is a hand made shoe.

Diet

Feeding during the fifth week takes on a new look too. With the concentrate ration up to 9 lbs for a sixteen hand horse, the feeds must now number four a day. This will mean the time at grass must be reduced by an hour to no more than three. Two in the morning and one in the afternoon. If there is a lot of grass on the field reduce it even more. My time at grass refers to a paddock that has been topped to three inches or less, or well grazed to this length.

36

Care & Management

The horse will now require re-shoeing. Feathered edged shoes are essential for the hind feet with quarter clips. Anything else and the horse could well strike into itself when moving at a faster pace.

Providing the exercise, feeding and grooming have been

12. Near-hind freshly re-shod. This too, is a hand made shoe with semi-feathered inside edge (full feathering brings the shoe in even narrower and the last nail by the heel is omitted), quarter clips at the toe to prevent the risk of over-reaching, the shoe being set behind the toe for added safety. The nails are well spaced and driven home so as to prevent the clenches rising once work is started. The new road stud is of the screw in type so that it can be inter-changed with jumping studs for competition work. This is a good, well made, safe shoe, with the heels well finished off—the type of shoe that is every horse's right. Thanks to good shoeing this is a healthy foot with a well formed frog capable of doing its job.

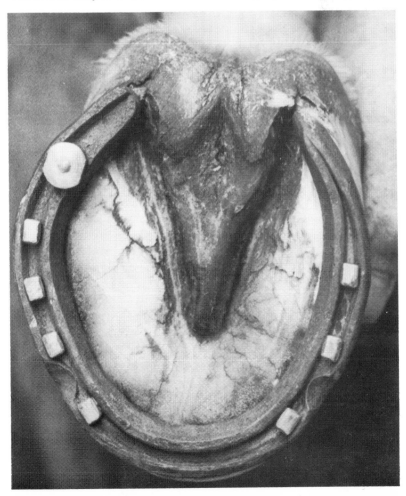

thorough during the preceding four weeks, the horse's coat should now really shine and move freely over muscles that are hardening well and beginning to bulge out above the forelegs and on the quarters. If a shine is not forthcoming, then something is amiss. Somewhere along the line either you have slipped up in your work, or else the horse has something wrong with it that cannot be seen. If the flesh is coming off rather than being converted into muscle, and the coat is staring, dull, dry and harsh to touch, then call in your veterinary surgeon. He will give the horse a thorough overhaul and check its lungs, heart and, if he thinks necessary, its blood and urine. It is useless to go on in the mistaken idea that all is well—all is not well in cases like this.

A fit horse is not necessarily a lean horse. Leanness often means food is being put into a bad skin; this is a waste, but often easily rectified if recognised in time. Sharp teeth, or worms can lie behind the poorness. A horse can be fit, hard and still big bodied; the difference is that with a fit horse the flesh is hard, the body outline trim, and the whole appearance is one of alertness. A fat, soft horse, on the other hand, is sleepy, and has its stomach well rounded in all directions as if it's let its stay-laces out.

Poorness can come from simply fretting and unhappiness either in its surroundings, or with its rider. This is often hard for the owner to see if they themselves are looking after the horse. A groom may get on well with one horse and another just fails to do so. This type of un-thriftiness can be suspected if the horse does well and picks up when one person is doing it and then promptly starts to revert to its former shadow when the original person takes over again.

A 'stitch in time saves nine' is only too true where horses are concerned, and if a horse is not doing as well as it should, then do try and find out why. It will never be really fit and hard if you do not. To say happily that 'so and so' horse has always had its ribs showing—is pure nonsense, it may well have, but I have proved time and again that it is quite unnecessary. No, a fit horse should have its ribs well covered and its whole body moulded into a well covered hard shape, in keeping with its conformation.

So much for the fifth week; by the end of it one should be able to have two or three short canters per session without the horse puffing too hard. Look now for plenty of slopes to trot up as the horse should now be trotting on with a swinging stride that really covers the ground in a smooth rhythm.

38

CHAPTER 8

Sixth week

Providing all is well with the horse at the start of the sixth week, then one can start to let the horse out a little when cantering, and enjoy a medium canter of a reasonable length. Do not over do it the first few days; but by the end of the week the horse should be able to have a reasonable canter without blowing, and have to be pulled up rather than come to a halt on its own account. When reducing speed, do so at a steady, balanced pace rather than 'jerking' it back to the slower speed. Gentle reduction of speed leads to far less risk of injury to tendons than a sudden one. Watch jockeys at the end of a race, seldom do they pull up quickly, but slow down by degrees. The faster one goes, the longer it takes to reduce speed and change pace. It is very like a car—drive too fast and then apply the brakes fiercely, trouble is sure to follow—both horse and car will slither to a halt.

Diet
Food will now have reached a reasonable ration and a sixteen hand horse should be getting 10 lbs of concentrate ration per day. What ration of nuts to oats one feeds depends very largely on the type of nuts being fed, and the horse. If proper horse nuts are being used—Racehorse or High Performance nuts of some sort, as they carry 14% protein—then the ratio could be 50-50, or .
I, in fact, like to use cattle rearing nuts as they carry a 15% to 16% protein. These I feed at the rate of 2 lbs nuts to 3 lbs oats, as they then make the total 5 lbs worth about the equivalent to 6 lbs of oats in food value.

If I am using flaked maize I substitute part of the nut ration with the maize, leaving the oats at the same rate. Increase the oats before the nuts if using cattle nuts, but with the other types of nuts it depends on the horse. If you cannot get the horse to eat a large amount of oats then it may be necessary to increase the nuts to make up the full ration, or to include a high protein supplement. Remember though, nuts are very dry and the horse will drink more water when being fed a large quantity of nuts. He needs this extra water to digest the nuts, otherwise they will impact within the stomach and trouble will follow.

Exercise

Work in sitting trot can now commence, but do not do it for too long the first few days—work up gradually. Once the horse is happy with a sitting trot—one of the best ways for bringing the hocks under the body and making the horse engage them properly, one can also include with advantage some time without ones stirrups. The object of doing this is to strengthen one's seat muscles, and get oneself deeper into the saddle. Five minutes the first day—by the end of the week one should be feeling quite at home without them. If one is a good rider and the horse quiet, then one can also work at the rising trot. Yes, it is quite possible to rise at the trot without stirrups and also without a saddle! The better the rider, the better for the horse in the weeks to come when it is really being called on to work.

Schooling

Schooling can now take on a more serious turn. Up till now one should only have been doing circles—fairly large ones, at a rising trot, and during the last week canters down the long sides of a school or outdoor arena, now one can introduce work at the sitting trot, close in the circles to that required in a dressage test, and also start cantering on the circle. With the latter do not overdo the first few days. Nothing is worse for the horse than to be kept at a thing for hours and hours till it is exhausted. This is when the muscles give and the horse goes lame. Once the horse is fully fit one can 'work' it properly, even then never to the point of exhaustion. Schooling is something a horse must enjoy, once they start fighting the rider in a dressage test, all your marks and that of your horse have vanished! Many horses are spoilt for dressage by over schooling in the days before they are physically fit enough to do what is asked of them. Pain from sore muscles is one of the quickest ways of making a horse frightened of doing a calm test.

Care & Management

Grooming, including strapping, now will be even more time consuming if the horse is to be got truly fit, taking at least half-an-hour longer than the half to three-quarters-of-an-hour required for the rest of the grooming. This strapping does pay dividends in muscle formation. Too, it gets the owner fit if they are strapping their own horse!

The conclusion of the sixth week sees the end of the third part of the getting fit programme—each two weeks forming a definite phase. Small horses with lighter frames may well be three parts fit now, or have reached the stage they can undertake moderately strenuous work for a short period of time, but their big brothers with bulkier frames will need another two weeks before going further than their home grounds and countryside.

CHAPTER 9

Seventh week

The seventh week sees the commencement of the final phase in the getting fit programme. This week and the following one are used as a build up to real work. Those horses you know can be got fit in eight weeks can now start their final preparation for competitions; others must wait till the full eight weeks have elapsed before doing their work up over the two weeks it takes to tune up.

When planning the competition programme, whether for a novice or experienced horse, never over enter during the early part of the season. One show or event a week or even a fortnight is quite enough when you first bring them out. This gives time to recover from one show before being rushed off to the next. Remember, travelling takes it out of many horses. If your horse is not used to travelling, then now is the time to bandage up and dress them fully for travelling, and take them off to some other part of the countryside for their exercise and work—providing you can get permission to ride on land in the district you wish to use. Do not go far—four or five miles will be far enough to start with. Drive considerately, being careful not to swing round corners, or throw them over when braking. Naturally if you do not own a trailer or box and have no ultra kind friend to lend you theirs, then this part of the preparation must be foregone. If one can do it the horse grows used to the movement of the box or trailer, and learns to use its legs to remain upright without risking the added strain of a full competition.

Travelling is tiring and many competitions have been lost through a horse having exhausted itself before ever starting. Bad travellers are a problem, but in many cases it can be overcome with time.

Another object of taking them to strange parts for their work is to get them used to unboxing with odd sounds and sights round them and not in the small confines of their own home. Some horses will work very well at home, do a good test and jump well, only to get het up at a show or event, or even out hunting, refusing to settle. Once a horse realizes nothing horrid is going to happen to it then most of them will settle and work normally.

Those whose work up to now has been on their own can with advantage be worked in company. This gets them used to others round them. Do not let them race each other when cantering, though canters can now speed up, and by the end of the week a short half-speed gallop can be included if one has a stretch of good sound going. On no account let the horse right out or let it get unbalanced.

Care & Management
Once this stage in the programme has been reached the horse will, even if nearly fit, be inclined to warm up or sweat. Up till now it should never have been worked to the point of sweating, even in the early days when it was completely soft. A rug at night, if not already worn, is now necessary to avoid chilling. In very warm weather use only a light one and put it on last thing, but in ordinary weather a normal night rug should not prove too warm. One does not want the horse to sweat in its box, being too warm is as bad as too cold, they need to be comfortable.

Jumping
Jumping can now be introduced to the day's work. Start with small jumps—the odd log out exercising and small jumps in the paddock at home. The object is to get the horse going freely forward and able to absorb any jar as it lands. Never ask them to jump full sized fences until they have had a week of small jumps, and do not jump more than four or six at a time to begin with. Remember every time they land they put a strain on their front legs, legs that must be given time to adjust themselves to the added strain and stretching involved. Over jump them at this stage and all those hours of slow work will have been wasted as the horse will be laid off and then you will have to start all over again!

CHAPTER 10

Eighth week

By now all one's hard work over the preceding weeks should be showing fruit and one's horse be very nearly fit and ready for hunting, one-day eventing, or sponsored rides, etc., in which the horse is called on to exert itself. It will be noticed that I have left out racing, three-day eventing and such activities that ask the horse to exert itself fast over a long period of time. For these another two to four weeks work is required to tune up to true pitch.

Diet

Between two and three hours steady exercise will now be required to keep the horse sober and his food will have reached the target of 12 lbs for the concentrate ration. Those called on for greater things will over the next two to four weeks increase even further if they can take it, to between 14 lbs and 16 lbs, according to size and temperament. But at this stage 12 lbs is really enough for a sixteen hand horse. Some may be happy on less and equally fit. All horses are individuals and have to be taken horse by horse when being fed.

Schooling

On the second day of the eighth week a half speed gallop can be included—on a gentle up hill slope of about half a mile for preference, to see if the horse is now breathing freely. If in any doubt, or the horse tries to slow, let it at this stage. The horse, unless born lazy, should be fully capable of knowing what it is ready for. Most are only too willing to sail on, and these have to be restrained. Once satisfied all is well, slow down to a steady canter, and then drop back to a trot, followed by a walk. Walk for the next mile or two and let the horse relax and cool off. Once cool and another mile or two has still to be covered, one can trot on again for another mile, and then walk the last mile back to the stable. *Always* walk the last mile home to cool off the horse. This is a rule that should only be broken in heavy, cold rain, when to walk would mean the horse would get chilled. Better then to bring them in warm so as to dry off the rain quicker.

Care & Management
The day following the gallop should be normal work that does not call for too much strain on the legs, and then on the fourth day another gallop can be given if the horse is going to run in an event on the sixth and last day of the week—the seventh day being the rest day.

With any luck the horse should now be fit enough to run without harm to itself. But do not be too over ambitious; do your dressage, and your show jumping if it is an event, but when it comes to the cross-country, first check the legs for coolness—this check must be made each night and morning incidentally—if cool and showing no signs of trouble go on to the cross-country, but with no aim of cutting down the seconds. Far, far better to have twenty, even fifty, penalty points for time than a lame horse with only one time fault. Time on these courses is fast and meant for the very fit, not those running for the first time of the season. Think of your horse and the ride will be all the more enjoyable. It is no credit to turn your horse over because it is not fit. This is how crashing falls occur—falls that could in many cases be avoided if the horse was not asked too much of it before it is ready. Far better to go slowly and still have a horse to ride the next time.

Hunting too, calls for a firm rider who knows when to go home. No credit is attached to riding all day only to have a horse drop from sheer exhaustion and lack of true fitness. The first few days after the eight weeks are over should be no more than half days or a couple of hours. Hunting calls for a very fit horse and until fully tuned up one must give it all the consideration it requires. In fact one must always put the welfare of one's horse before one's own pleasure.

By the end of the eighth week the shoes will require renewing again. This time shoes suitable for the work required must be fitted—screw in stud holes for those whose shoes have to carry jumping studs.

Well, I hope the long slog has been worth it, and if it has seemed long and drawn out, then that is what I intended it to be in order to give some impression of how long it takes to get a horse really fit.

CHAPTER 11

Exercise versus work

Having now got the average sixteen hand horse fit enough to undertake real work, it is as well to understand the difference between work and exercise.

Exercise consists of giving the horse the necessary amount of walking and trotting to keep its muscles in tune and prevent it from becoming above itself from sheer high spirits but without tiring it.

Work, on the other hand, is when we ride for the pleasure of it, and go out with the object of having a 'good' ride. By a good ride I mean the odd canter, slow gallop, if the going is good, a jolly across country if one has some sound, safe fences to jump. In short, the horse and rider do not mind if they get a bit muddy and tired, providing they have both had a good time. Hunting, hacking on the above lines, schooling, long distance riding, sponsored rides, trekking, eventing, hunter trials, show jumping, showing, polo, racing—these are all labelled as work. Work calls for stress and strain and should not be done every day, although a riding school horse will have to earn its keep by working six days out of seven (no school should work a horse or pony for seven days a week).

On the days when a horse is not being called on to work in the above sense, then it must be properly exercised, either by its owner or by someone capable of riding a fit horse in a sensible manner. If ridden exercise is not possible for some reason, then the horse must be exercised by some other means. It can be led from another horse, in which case it must be placed on the near (left) side, between the ridden horse and the curb, and if clipped be wearing a rug. Always ride with the traffic and know the highway code. Lungeing is another means of exercising a fit horse. Use a proper lungeing cavesson and rein as it is much safer than lungeing either off the bit—never to be encouraged as the mouth can so easily be damaged this way, or from an ordinary headcollar. For some, exercising means an hour's walk in-hand with the leader on foot. When walking on foot it is permissible to lead a horse against the traffic, but you must be between the horse and the traffic. Failing all else the horse can be turned out for an hour or two to exercise itself. In winter with a New Zealand rug on. In summer, without a rug.

The time at grass, once a horse is fit, should be cut to about an hour, or curtailed completely with grazing walks substituted if the weather is nice and warm. Too much grass takes up room in their stomachs that is required for hard food. An hour's grazing though is not enough to do this, and lets the horse relax, relieving its boredom—boredom from which can stem stable vices like weaving, crib-biting, windsucking, chewing of wood—all of which do the horse no good, and can effect its condition.

The amount of exercise required once a horse is fit depends on how hard it is working. The day after hard work the horse requires a leg stretch, but on ordinary days about one-and-a-half to two hours are necessary. If no fast work has been done for four or five days, or even a week, and is not going to be done within the next two, then the horse must be given a good long exercise of three hours and about fifteen miles. When working hard regularly then these long rides are not necessary. It must be remebered that the horse is being fed for hard work and if it is not exercised properly it will not only get above itself, but its health will suffer from too much protein with not enough work to burn it up. Adjust feed to work, but remember it is far better to exercise well and feed well, than to cut off the food once the horse is fit.

If someone else is exercising your horse it is wise to know just what time a certain circuit takes at a reasonable pace. Any time under this means that the rider is either cutting short the exercise or bashing on too fast—both bad. On the other hand if the rider is taking too long over a given circuit, then they are either ambling along and not exercising properly, or else stopping and talking. If the horse is wearing a rug this is one thing, but if not, in winter, a chill could set in and trouble will soon tell the truth!

Plan your routes for exercising; know how long it takes for each at a given pace or combination of paces, and work out your routine from these according to how much exercise the horse requires on a given day.

CHAPTER 12

Care while in full work

Once the horse is fit, the main object is to keep it so. Stable routine plays a large part in the care of the fit horse. I personally like to start my stables early in the morning between 6 am and 6.30 am. The reason for this is, should the horse have become ill in the night with colic or something else, then one finds it as early as possible and can do something quickly. Admittedly it is too early to phone the veterinary surgeon, except in extreme cases, but one can watch the horse and do whatever is in one's own power while waiting for a reasonable hour. If the horse is really ill, then one must phone and no good veterinary surgeon will mind. Time in some cases is vital. If on the other hand one drifts down to the stables sometime after 7.30 am, or even later, then the horse can have been ill for some considerable time without help. Even the best run stables get trouble at times, so an early start helps.

An early start also makes fitting in the feeds much easier and the horse has plenty of time to digest its feed before exercise.

Clean stables are essential to health. Everything should be done thoroughly, either by the owner, or whoever is responsible for the work. The Master's Eye is the best thing around provided the master knows what is required. If you want to keep your horse fit, then go to the trouble of learning how, and setting yourself and your staff a high standard. Carelessness only leads to injury and other troubles that can spoil all the hours of hard work getting the horse fit.

Good, clean stables that have had all the bed lifted each morning, the floor swept and then re-bedded with plenty of clean fresh straw on top; plenty of fresh water in a clean bucket always to hand; good food, well prepared in clean buckets, and given in a clean manger; ample, steady exercise to keep the horse happy and sober; thorough grooming with clean grooming kit; shoeing every four to five weeks with shoes of the correct weight and fit; and kind, firm handling all go to produce and keep a horse happy and content. A credit to its owner and pleasure to ride and own.